THE CROSS AND THE EMPTY TOMB

MEDITATIONS ON EASTER AND THE RESURRECTION

Copyright 2023 by Smith-Freeman Publishing.
The Cross and the Empty Tomb: Meditations on Easter and the Resurrection

All rights reserved. No part of this book may be reproduced, stored in a retrieval system, or transmitted in any form or by any means—electronic, mechanical, photocopying, recording, or any other—except for brief quotations in printed reviews, without prior written permission of the publisher.

The quoted ideas expressed in this book (but not Scripture verses) are not, in all cases, exact quotations, as some have been edited for clarity and brevity. In all cases, the author has attempted to maintain the speaker's original intent. In some cases, quoted material for this book was obtained from secondary sources, primarily print media. Every effort was made to ensure the accuracy of these sources.

Bible verses were taken from the following translations:

Scripture quotations marked (HCSB) are taken from the Holman Christian Standard Bible®, Copyright © 1999, 2000, 2002, 2003, 2009 Holman Bible Publishers. Used by Permission. Holman Christian Standard Bible®, Holman CSB®, and HCSB® are federally registered trademarks of Holman Bible Publishers.

Scripture quotations marked (KJV) are from the King James Version. Public domain.

Scripture quotations marked (MSG) are taken from THE MESSAGE, copyright © 1993, 2002, 2018 by Eugene H. Peterson. Used by permission of NavPress. All rights reserved. Represented by Tyndale House Publishers, a Division of Tyndale House Ministries.

Scripture quotations marked (NASB) are taken from the New American Standard Bible®, Copyright © 1960, 1971, 1977, 1995, 2020 by The Lockman Foundation. Used by permission. All rights reserved. lockman.org

Scripture quotations marked (NIV) are taken from the Holy Bible, New International Version®, NIV®. Copyright © 1973, 1978, 1984, 2011 by Biblica, Inc.™ Used by permission of Zondervan. All rights reserved worldwide. www.zondervan.com The "NIV" and "New International Version" are trademarks registered in the United States Patent and Trademark Office by Biblica, Inc.™

Scripture quotations marked (NKJV) are taken from the New King James Version®. Copyright © 1982 by Thomas Nelson. Used by permission. All rights reserved.

Scripture quotations marked (NLT) are taken from the Holy Bible, New Living Translation, copyright © 1996, 2004, 2015 by Tyndale House Foundation. Used by permission of Tyndale House Publishers, Inc, Carol Stream, Illinois 60188. All rights reserved.

Cover design by Kim Russell | Wahoo Designs

ISBN: 979-8-9872584-4-6

CONTENTS

A Message to Readers 4

PART I: The Cross 7

1. A Child Is Born 9
2. He Walked Among Us 15
3. A Servant's Heart 21
4. No Greater Love 27

PART II: The Empty Tomb 33

5. Not My Will, but Thine 35
6. It Is Finished 41
7. He Is Risen! 47

PART III: And We Shall Also Live 53

8. And We Shall Also Live 55
9. Building Upon the Rock 61
10. The Abundant Life 69
11. Ultimate Peace 73
12. Sharing the Good News 79
13. A Time for Celebration 85
14. A Time for Praise 89

A MESSAGE TO READERS

A hymn by Fanny Crosby contains this familiar refrain: "Tell me the story of Jesus." That story, of course, is one that we cannot tell—*or* hear—too often. This text contains fourteen chapters that examine the life, the death, and the resurrection of Jesus. These meditations are comprised of Bible verses, quotations from notable Christian thinkers, brief essays, and prayers.

Each year, on Good Friday, we commemorate Christ's sacrifice on the cross. And then, on Easter Sunday, we celebrate His victory over death: the empty tomb. It is on these two days that we can, and should, focus our thoughts and prayers on the life, the death, and the resurrection of God's only begotten Son.

Jesus is the sovereign friend and ultimate savior of mankind. Christ showed enduring love for His believers by willingly sacrificing His own life so that we might have eternal life. Now it is our turn to return His love by inviting Him into our hearts and sharing His message with the world.

Why did Christ endure the humiliation and torture of the cross? He did it for you. His love is as near as your next breath, as personal as your next thought, more essential than your next heartbeat. And what must you do in response to the Savior's gifts? You must accept His love, praise His name, and share His message of salvation. And you must conduct yourself in a manner that demonstrates to all the world that your acquaintance with Jesus is not a passing fancy but that it is, instead, the cornerstone and the touchstone of your life—today, tomorrow, and forever.

HE IS RISEN!

Now on the first day of the week, very early in the morning, they, and certain other women with them, came to the tomb bringing the spices which they had prepared. But they found the stone rolled away from the tomb. Then they went in and did not find the body of the Lord Jesus. And it happened, as they were greatly perplexed about this, that behold, two men stood by them in shining garments. Then, as they were afraid and bowed their faces to the earth, they said to them, "Why do you seek the living among the dead? He is not here, but is risen!"

Luke 24:1–6 NKJV

PART I:

THE CROSS

Praise be to the God and Father of our Lord Jesus Christ! In his great mercy he has given us new birth into a living hope through the resurrection of Jesus Christ from the dead, and into an inheritance that can never perish, spoil or fade.

1 Peter 1:3-4 NIV

1
A CHILD IS BORN

*For unto you is born this day in the city of
David a Saviour, which is Christ the Lord.*

Luke 2:11 KJV

He was the Son of God, but He wore a crown of thorns. He was the savior of mankind, yet He was put to death on a rough-hewn cross made of wood. He offered His healing touch to an unsaved world, and yet the same hands that had healed the sick and raised the dead were pierced with nails.

Jesus Christ, the Son of God, was born into humble circumstances. He walked this earth, not as a ruler of men, but as the Savior of mankind. His crucifixion, a torturous punishment that was intended to end His life and His reign, instead became the pivotal event in human history.

Each year at Easter, we celebrate the death and

resurrection of our Savior. May we, the recipients of Christ's grace, remember the gravity of His sacrifice. Christ wore the crown of thorns and endured the pain of the cross for each of us.

Two thousand years ago, God sent His Son to transform the world and to save it. God's Son was born in a nondescript village, to parents of simple means, far from the seats of earthy power.

> *And it came to pass in those days, that there went out a decree from Caesar Augustus that all the world should be taxed . . . . And all went to be taxed, every one into his own city. And Joseph also went up from Galilee, out of the city of Nazareth, into Judaea, unto the city of David, which is called Bethlehem; (because he was of the house and lineage of David) to be taxed with Mary his espoused wife, being great with child. And so it was, that, while they were there, the days were accomplished that she should be delivered. And she brought forth her firstborn son, and wrapped him in swaddling clothes, and laid him in a manger; because there was no room for them in the inn. And there were in the same country shepherds abiding in the field, keeping watch over their flock by night. And, lo, the angel of the Lord*

came upon them, and the glory of the Lord shone round about them; and they were sore afraid. And the angel said unto them, Fear not: for, behold, I bring you good tidings of great joy, which shall be to all people. For unto you is born this day in the city of David a Saviour, which is Christ the Lord. And this shall be a sign unto you; Ye shall find the babe wrapped in swaddling clothes, lying in a manger. And suddenly there was with the angel a multitude of the heavenly host praising God, and saying, Glory to God in the highest, and on earth peace, good will toward men.

Luke 2:1–14 KJV

The Christ child changed the world forever, and He can do the same for us. We, like shepherds tending our fields, are busy tending to the demands of daily life. But as we carve out time to worship Him, we must leave our duties behind, at least for a while, so that we may celebrate the One who has saved us.

Let us celebrate Jesus: His birth, His life, His death, and His resurrection. Let us praise Him for His peace and His love. May we, like those shepherds of old, leave our fields—wherever they may be—and pause to worship God's priceless gift: His only begotten Son.

To God be the glory, great things He has done;
So loved He the world that He gave us His Son.

Fanny Crosby

Jesus Christ was born into this world, not from it.

Oswald Chambers

In the beginning was the Word, and the Word was with God, and the Word was God. . . . And the Word was made flesh, and dwelt among us, (and we beheld his glory, the glory as of the only begotten of the Father,) full of grace and truth.

John 1:1,14 KJV

The central message of the Bible is Jesus Christ.

Billy Graham

In every Christian, Christ lives again. Every true
believer is a return to first-century Christianity.

VANCE HAVNER

I have a great need for Christ;
I have a great Christ for my need.

C. H. SPURGEON

For the Christ-child who comes is the Master of all;
No palace too great, no cottage too small.

PHILLIPS BROOKS

Good news from heaven the angels bring,
glad tidings to the earth they sing:
To us this day a child is given,
to crown us with the joy of heaven.

MARTIN LUTHER

*Jesus said unto them, Verily, verily, I say
unto you, Before Abraham was, I am.*
JOHN 8:58 KJV

*At the name of Jesus every knee should bow,
of things in heaven, and things in earth,
and things under the earth; and that every
tongue should confess that Jesus Christ
is Lord, to the glory of God the Father.*
PHILIPPIANS 2:10–11 KJV

A PRAYER

Dear Lord, keep me mindful of Your priceless gift: my personal Savior, Christ Jesus. Father, You loved me before I was ever born, and You will love me throughout eternity. In return, let me offer my life to You so that I might live according to Your commandments and according to Your plan. Today and every day, I will praise You, Lord, as I give thanks for Your Son Jesus and for Your everlasting love. Amen

2
HE WALKED AMONG US

*I have set you an example that
you should do as I have done for you.*

JOHN 13:15 NIV

During the Easter season—and during every other season of the year—we must remember that Jesus was —and is—God's unique gift to the world.

How marvelous it is that God's only begotten Son became a man and walked among us. Had the Lord not chosen to do so, we might feel removed from a distant Creator. But ours is not a distant God. Ours is a God who understands—far better than we ever could—the essence of what it means to be human.

God understands our hopes, our fears, and our temptations. He understands what it means to be angry and what it costs to forgive. He knows the heart, the conscience, and the soul of every person who has ever lived, including you. And God has a plan of salvation that is intended for you. Accept it. Accept God's gift through the person of His Son, and then rest assured: God walked among us so that you might have eternal life. Amazing though it may seem, He did it for you.

> We say that Jesus preached the gospel, but he did more. He came that there might be a gospel to preach.
> OSWALD CHAMBERS

> The King of kings and Lord of lords, the only Begotten of the Father was born in a stable, raised by a poor carpenter, teased by his brothers, and was virtually homeless, practically penniless. He was deserted by his friends, insulted in a kangaroo court, mocked, beaten, stripped, bruised, then crucified. To us it is a scenario that makes little sense. To God it was the only scenario that made any sense.
> BETH MOORE

> Christ knows better than you what it means to be human.
> JONI EARECKSON TADA

Here is our opportunity: we cannot see God, but we
can see Christ. Christ was not only the Son of God, but
He was the Father. Whatever Christ was, that God is.

Hannah Whitall Smith

When you are weary and everything seems
to be going wrong, you can still utter these
four words: "I trust You, Jesus."

Sarah Young

Christ's excellency is always fresh and new, and
it delights as much after it has been seen for ten
thousand years as when it was seen the first moment.

Jonathan Edwards

Christians are not citizens of earth trying
to get to heaven, but citizens of heaven
making their way through this world.

Vance Havner

Tell me the story of Jesus. Write on my
heart every word. Tell me the story most
precious, sweetest that ever was heard.

Fanny Crosby

The Scriptures are in print what Christ is in person.
A. W. Tozer

Once we recognize our need for Jesus, then the building of our faith begins. It is a daily, moment-by-moment life of absolute dependence upon Him for everything.
Catherine Marshall

Learn to keep close to Jesus, to listen to His voice, and to follow Him.
Billy Graham

Jesus—the standard of measurement, the scale of weights, the test of character for the whole moral universe.
R. G. Lee

He became what we are that he might make us what he is.
St. Athanasius

Christ, the Son of God, the complete embodiment of God's Word, came among us. He looked on humanity's losing battle with sin and pitched His divine tent in the middle of the camp so that He could dwell among us.
Beth Moore

The amazing thing about Jesus is that He doesn't just patch up our lives, He gives us a brand new sheet, a clean slate to start over, all new.
Gloria Gaither

This is my song through endless ages: Jesus led me all the way.
Fanny Crosby

Jesus departed from our sight that he might return to our hearts. He departed, and behold, he is here.
St. Augustine

The Son is the image of the invisible God, the firstborn over all creation. For in him all things were created: things in heaven and on earth, visible and invisible, whether thrones or powers or rulers or authorities; all things have been created through him and for him.
Colossians 1:15–16 NIV

*For the Son of Man came to seek
and to save what was lost.*

Luke 19:10 NIV

*And surely I am with you always,
to the very end of the age.*

Matthew 28:20 NIV

A PRAYER

Dear Lord, You sent Your Son to die on a cross so that I might have eternal life. And because Jesus was a man who walked this earth, You possess a perfect understanding of all humanity, including my own frailties and shortcomings. I praise you, Lord, for Your love, for Your forgiveness, for Your grace, and for Your Son. Let me share the good news of Jesus Christ, the One who became a man so that I might become His, not only for today, but also for all eternity.

3
A SERVANT'S HEART

*But whosoever will be great among you,
let him be your minister; and whosoever
will be chief among you, let him be your
servant: even as the Son of man came
not to be ministered unto, but to minister,
and to give his life a ransom for many.*

Matthew 20:26–28 KJV

How do we achieve greatness in the eyes of God? By accumulating wealth? Or acquiring power? Or by gaining fame, popularity, or prestige? Of course not. We achieve greatness in God's eyes by serving His children gladly, humbly, and often.

Everywhere we look, the needs are great. Whether here at home or halfway around the globe, so many people are enduring difficult circumstances. They our need help, and as Christians, we are instructed to serve them.

If you genuinely seek to discover God's unfolding purpose for your life, you must ask yourself this question: How does God want me to serve? Whatever your path, whatever your calling, you may be certain of this: service to others is an integral part of God's plan for you.

Every day of your life, including this one, the Lord will give you opportunities to serve Him by serving His children. Welcome those opportunities with open arms. They are God's gift to you, His way of allowing you to achieve greatness in His kingdom.

Jesus came to this world, not to conquer, but to serve. We must do likewise by helping those who cannot help themselves. When we do, our lives will be blessed by the One who first served us.

> In Jesus, the service of God and the service
> of the least of the brethren were one.
> DIETRICH BONHOEFFER

> Holy service in constant fellowship
> with God is heaven below.
> C. H. SPURGEON

> Before the judgment seat of Christ, my service
> will not be judged by how much I have done
> but by how much of me there is in it.
> A. W. TOZER

It is the duty of every Christian to
be Christ to his neighbor.

MARTIN LUTHER

You can judge how far you have risen in the scale
of life by asking one question: How wisely and
how deeply do I care? To be Christianized is to
be sensitized. Christians are people who care.

E. STANLEY JONES

Do all the good you can, by all the means you
can, in all the ways you can, in all the places
you can, at all the times you can, to all the
people you can, as long as ever you can.

JOHN WESLEY

No life can surpass that of a man who
quietly continues to serve God in the place
where providence has placed him.

C. H. SPURGEON

Only God's chosen task for you will ultimately satisfy.
Do not wait until it is too late to realize the privilege
of serving Him in His chosen position for you.

BETH MOORE

We do the works, but God works in
us in the doing of the works.
St. Augustine

Selfishness is as far from Christianity
as darkness is from light.
C. H. Spurgeon

God wants us to serve Him with a willing spirit,
one that would choose no other way.
Beth Moore

Abundant living means abundant giving.
E. Stanley Jones

Giving to God and, in His name, to others, is not
something that we do; it the result of what we are.
Warren Wiersbe

The goodness you receive from God is a
treasure for you to share with others.
Elizabeth George

What does love look like? It has the hands to help others. It has the feet to hasten to the poor and needy. It has eyes to see misery and want. It has the ears to hear the sighs and sorrows of men. That is what love looks like.

St. Augustine

For it is in giving that we receive.

St. Francis of Assisi

A true servant of God is one who helps another succeed.

Billy Graham

The measure of a life, after all, is not its duration but its donation.

Corrie ten Boom

It is one of the most beautiful compensations of life that no one can sincerely try to help another without helping herself.

Barbara Johnson

Christian life consists in faith and charity.

Martin Luther

Freely you have received; freely give.

MATTHEW 10:8 NIV

Truly I tell you, whatever you did for one of the least of these brothers and sisters of mine, you did for me.

MATTHEW 25:40 NIV

A PRAYER

Father in heaven, when Jesus humbled Himself and became a servant, He also became an example for His followers. Today, as I serve my family and friends, I do so in the name of Jesus, my Lord and Master. Guide my steps, Father, and let my service be pleasing to You. Amen

4
NO GREATER LOVE . . .

*Greater love has no one than this: to
lay down one's life for one's friends.*

JOHN 15:13 NIV

How much does Christ love us? More than we, as mere mortals, can comprehend. His love is perfect and steadfast. Even though we are fallible and wayward, the Good Shepherd cares for us still. Even though we have fallen far short of the Father's commandments, Christ loves us with a power and depth that is beyond our understanding. The sacrifice that Jesus made upon the cross was made for each of us, and His love endures to the edge of eternity and beyond.

During the Easter season, we are reminded, yet again, that Christ's love changes everything. When we accept His gift of grace, we are transformed, not only for today, but forever. Yes, Christ's love changes everything. May we invite Him into our hearts so it can then change everything *in us*.

> Christ's excellency is always fresh and new, and it delights as much after it has been seen for ten thousand years as when it was seen the first moment.
> JONATHAN EDWARDS

> Lord, I am no longer my own, but Yours. Put me to what You will, rank me with whom You will. Let me be employed by You or laid aside for You, exalted for You or brought low by You. Let me have all things, let me have nothing. I freely and heartily yield all things to Your pleasure and disposal. And now, O glorious and blessed God, Father, Son, and Holy Spirit, You are mine and I am Yours. So be it. Amen.
> JOHN WESLEY

> In his life, Christ is an example showing us how to live; in his death, he is a sacrifice satisfying for our sins.
> MARTIN LUTHER

The love of God is one of the great realities
of the universe, a pillar upon which the hope
of the world rests. But it is a personal, intimate
thing too. God does not love populations. He
loves people. He loves not masses, but men.

A. W. TOZER

Almost 2000 years ago, Jesus Christ won the decisive
battle against sin and Satan through His death and
resurrection. Satan did his best to defeat God's plans,
but he could not win against God's overwhelming power.

BILLY GRAHAM

Begin to know Him now, and finish never.

OSWALD CHAMBERS

Christ's reign in His church is that of shepherd-king.
He has supremacy, but it is the superiority of a wise
and tender shepherd over His needy and loving flock;
He commands and receives obedience, but it is willing
obedience of well-cared-for sheep, offered joyfully to
their beloved Shepherd, whose voice they know so well.
He rules by the force of love and the energy of goodness.

C. H. SPURGEON

Our Lord has written the promise of the resurrection,
not in books alone, but in every leaf in spring-time.

MARTIN LUTHER

Christianity is a love relationship between a child
of God and his Maker through the Son Jesus
Christ and in the power of the Holy Spirit.

ADRIAN ROGERS

He loved us not because we're
lovable, but because He is love.

C. S. LEWIS

Christ is not valued at all unless He is valued above all.

ST. AUGUSTINE

Jesus is all compassion. He never betrays us.

CATHERINE MARSHALL

Jesus Christ is the first and last, author and finisher, beginning and end, alpha and omega, and by Him all other things hold together. He must be first or nothing. God never comes next!

Vance Havner

For I am convinced that neither death, nor life, nor angels, nor principalities, nor things present, nor things to come, nor powers, nor height, nor depth, nor any other created thing, will be able to separate us from the love of God, which is in Christ Jesus our Lord.
ROMANS 8:38–39 NASB 1995

For while we were still helpless, at the appointed moment, Christ died for the ungodly.
ROMANS 5:6 HCSB 1995

Jesus Christ is the same yesterday and today and forever.
HEBREWS 13:8 NASB 1995

A PRAYER

Dear Jesus, I am humbled by Your love and mercy. You when to Calvary so that I might have eternal life. Thank You, Jesus, for Your priceless gift, and for Your love. You loved me first, Lord, and I will return Your love today, tomorrow, and forever. Amen

PART II:
THE EMPTY TOMB

Now upon the first day of the week, very early in the morning, they came unto the sepulchre, bringing the spices which they had prepared, and certain others with them. And they found the stone rolled away from the sepulchre. And they entered in, and found not the body of the Lord Jesus.

Luke 24:1–3 KJV

The story of Easter is the story of an empty tomb. It is a story of betrayal, suffering, and death followed by resurrection, rejoicing, and eternal life. The story of Easter is God's message to the world that through Him we can—indeed we must— have hope. The story of Easter is the story of God's love, God's miracles, and God's offer of salvation.

Christ died so that we might have spiritual abundance, earthly peace, and eternal life. As we consider the empty tomb and all that it signifies, let us praise the Father and the Son for gifts that are too numerous to count, too profound to understand, and too costly to ever take for granted.

5
NOT MY WILL, BUT THINE

And he was withdrawn from them about a stone's cast, and kneeled down, and prayed, saying, Father, if thou be willing, remove this cup from me: nevertheless not my will, but thine, be done. And there appeared an angel unto him from heaven, strengthening him. And being in an agony he prayed more earnestly: and his sweat was as it were great drops of blood falling down to the ground.

Luke 22:41–44 KJV

When Jesus confronted the reality of His impending death on the cross, He asked God that this terrible burden might be lifted. But as He faced the possibility of a suffering that was beyond description, Jesus prayed, "Nevertheless not my will, but thine, be done." As Christians, we, too, must be willing to accept God's will, even when we do not fully understand the reasons for the hardships, the setbacks, and the heartbreaks that all of us must occasionally endure.

Grief and suffering visit all of us who live long and love deeply. When we lose a loved one, or when we experience any other profound loss, darkness overwhelms us for a while, and it seems as if we cannot summon the strength to face another day. But with God's help, we can.

When we confront circumstances that trouble us to the very core of our souls, we must trust God. When we are worried, we must turn our concerns over to Him. When we are anxious, we must be still and listen for the quiet assurance of God's promises. And then, by placing our lives in His hands, we learn that He is our shepherd today and throughout eternity.

> If there is something we need more than anything else during grief, it is a friend who stands with us, who doesn't leave us. Jesus is that friend.
> BILLY GRAHAM

> The Almighty does nothing without reason, although the frail mind of man cannot explain the reason.
> ST. AUGUSTINE

> God does not give us everything we want, but He does fulfill all His promises as He leads us along the best and straightest paths to Himself.
> DIETRICH BONHOEFFER

God is at work; He is in full control; He is in the midst of
whatever has happened, is happening, and will happen.

CHARLES SWINDOLL

The God who orchestrates the universe has a good
many things to consider that have not occurred
to me, and it is well that I leave them to Him.

ELISABETH ELLIOT

In God's economy, whether He is making a flower or
a human soul, nothing ever comes to nothing. The
losses are His way of accomplishing the gains.

ELISABETH ELLIOT

Letting God have His way can be an uncomfortable thing.

CHARLES SWINDOLL

Your will should be corrected to become identified with
God's will. You must not bend God's will to suit yours.

ST. AUGUSTINE

The only thing that can hinder us is our own
failure to work in harmony with the plans
of the Creator, and if this lack of harmony
can be removed, then God can work.

HANNAH WHITALL SMITH

The geography and the details of His plan will be different for each one of us, of course, but the Spirit's sovereign working is far beyond what the human mind can ever imagine (Isaiah 55:8–9).

CHARLES SWINDOLL

Put your hand into the hand of God. He gives the calmness and serenity of heart and soul.

LETTIE COWMAN

God's goal is not to make you happy. It is to make you his.

MAX LUCADO

I thought God's purpose was to make me full of happiness and joy. It is, but it is happiness and joy from God's standpoint, not from mine.

OSWALD CHAMBERS

When a train goes through a tunnel and it gets
dark, you don't throw away your ticket and
jump off. You sit still and trust the engineer.

CORRIE TEN BOOM

It is possible to see God's will in every circumstance
and to accept it with singing instead of complaining.

LETTIE COWMAN

Never be afraid to trust an unknown
future to a known God.

CORRIE TEN BOOM

Never yield to gloomy anticipation. Place your hope
and confidence in God. He has no record of failure.

LETTIE COWMAN

*Trust in the L̲o̲r̲d̲ with all thine heart;
and lean not unto thine own understanding. In all thy ways acknowledge
him, and he shall direct thy paths.*

PROVERBS 3:5–6 KJV

In thee, O L̲o̲r̲d̲, do I put my trust.

PSALM 31:1 KJV

*After this manner therefore pray
ye:. . . Thy kingdom come, Thy will
be done in earth, as it is in heaven.*

MATTHEW 6:9–10 KJV

A PRAYER

Dear Lord, let Your will be my will. When I am confused, give me maturity and wisdom. When I am worried, give me courage and strength. When I have doubts, keep me mindful of Your promises and let me trust You to fulfill them. Let me be Your faithful servant, Father, always seeking Your guidance and Your will for my life. Amen

6
IT IS FINISHED

After this, Jesus, knowing that all things had already been accomplished, to fulfill the Scripture, said, "I am thirsty." A jar full of sour wine was standing there; so they put a sponge full of the sour wine upon a branch of hyssop and brought it up to His mouth. Therefore when Jesus had received the sour wine, He said, "It is finished!" And He bowed His head and gave up His spirit.

JOHN 19:28–30 NASB

On a Friday morning, on a hill outside the walls of Jerusalem, Jesus was crucified. Darkness came over the land, the curtain of the temple was torn in two, and finally Jesus called out, "Father, into your hands I commit my spirit" (Luke 23:46 NIV). Christ had endured the crucifixion, and now it was finished.

The body of Jesus was wrapped in a linen shroud and placed in a new tomb. It was there that God breathed life into His Son. It was there that Christ was resurrected. It was there that the angels rejoiced. And as believers who seek to follow in the footsteps of God's resurrected Son, we must rejoice too.

> It is because of God's loving grace that Jesus died on the cross for our sins so we could experience an eternal relationship with Him.
>
> BILL BRIGHT

> Christ is no Moses, no exactor, no giver of laws, but a giver of grace, a Savior; he is infinite mercy and goodness, freely and bountifully given to us.
>
> MARTIN LUTHER

> God proved his love on the cross. When Christ hung, and bled, and died it was God saying to the world—I love you.
>
> BILLY GRAHAM

The spectacle of the Cross, the most public event of Jesus' life, reveals the vast difference between a god who proves himself through power and One who proves himself through love.

PHILIP YANCEY

In the wounds of the dying Savior,
see the love of the great I AM.

C. H. SPURGEON

Jesus: the proof of God's love.

PHILIP YANCEY

The greatest love of all is God's love for us, a love that showed itself in action.

BILLY GRAHAM

The death of Christ is a wellspring of joy.

C. H. SPURGEON

Costly grace is the treasure hidden in the field; for the sake of it, a man will gladly go and sell all that he has. It is costly because it costs a man his life, and it is grace because it gives a man the only true life.

DIETRICH BONHOEFFER

Grace: a gift that costs everything for the giver and nothing for the recipient.

PHILIP YANCEY

There is no greater joy than the peace and assurance of knowing that, whatever the future may hold, you are secure in the loving arms of the Savior.

BILLY GRAHAM

The grace of God is sufficient for all our needs, for every problem, and for every difficulty, for every broken heart, and for every human sorrow.
PETER MARSHALL

The grace of God is infinite and eternal. As it had no beginning, so it can have no end, and being an attribute of God, it is as boundless as infinitude.
A. W. TOZER

Salvation comes through a cross and a crucified Christ.
ANDREW MURRAY

When you live in the light of eternity, your values change.
RICK WARREN

But we see Jesus, who was made a little lower than the angels for the suffering of death, crowned with glory and honour; that he by the grace of God should taste death for every man.
HEBREWS 2:9 KJV

I am the good shepherd: the good shepherd giveth his life for the sheep.
JOHN 10:11 KJV

Thanks be to God for his indescribable gift!
2 CORINTHIANS 9:15 NIV

A PRAYER

Dear Jesus, You gave Your life for me. Your love is boundless, infinite, and eternal. Today, let me pause and reflect upon Your sacrifice, Your gift of grace, and Your love. Amen

7
HE IS RISEN!

But very early on Sunday morning the women went to the tomb, taking the spices they had prepared. They found that the stone had been rolled away from the entrance. So they went in, but they didn't find the body of the Lord Jesus. As they stood there puzzled, two men suddenly appeared to them, clothed in dazzling robes. The women were terrified and bowed with their faces to the ground. Then the men asked, "Why are you looking among the dead for someone who is alive? He isn't here! He is risen from the dead!"

LUKE 24:1–6 NLT

It was strict adherence to Jewish law that prevented Jesus's followers from returning to His tomb on the Sabbath day (the first day after His death). So it was not until Sunday morning that a small band of beleaguered disciples journeyed to the tomb in order to care for the body of their beloved teacher. But when they arrived, the tomb was empty. Jesus was gone. Angels proclaimed the glorious news: Jesus had risen from the dead.

Christ's resurrection is the cornerstone upon which the Christian faith is built. The resurrection gives hope and assurance to all of us who accept Jesus as our Lord and Savior. Because the Savior was raised from the dead, so, too, may we have the gift of eternal life *if* we believe in Him. The joy of the Easter message is as simple as it is profound: The tomb is empty. The Savior lives. God's promise is fulfilled.

> If only we would stop lamenting and look up, God is here. Christ is risen. The Spirit has been poured out from on high.
> A. W. TOZER

> A child of God should be a visible beatitude for joy and a living doxology for gratitude.
> C. H. SPURGEON

> Let us see the victorious Jesus, the conqueror of the tomb, the one who defied death. And let us be reminded that we, too, will be granted the same victory.
> MAX LUCADO

Christ is risen! Hallelujah!
Gladness fills the world today;
From the tomb that
could not hold Him,
See, the stone is rolled away!

FANNY CROSBY

The redemption, accomplished for us by our Lord
Jesus Christ on the cross at Calvary, is redemption
from the power of sin as well as from its guilt. Christ
is able to save all who come unto God by Him.

Hannah Whitall Smith

*Blessed be the God and Father of our Lord Jesus
Christ, who according to His great mercy has
caused us to be born again to a living hope through
the resurrection of Jesus Christ from the dead.*

1 Peter 1:3 NASB

The way to be saved is not to delay,
but to come and take.

D. L. Moody

There is no one so far lost that Jesus
cannot find him and cannot save him.

Andrew Murray

The work of Jesus is the creation of saints.

Oswald Chambers

The Gospel is not so much a demand as it is an offer,
an offer of new life to man by the grace of God.

E. Stanley Jones

Good Friday and Easter free us to think about other things far beyond our own personal fate, about the ultimate meaning of all life, suffering, and events; and we lay hold of a great hope.

Dietrich Bonhoeffer

*He was raised on the third day
according to the Scriptures.*
1 CORINTHIANS 15:4 NASB

*Everyone who calls on the name
of the Lord will be saved.*
ROMANS 10:13 NIV

*Very truly I tell you, the one
who believes has eternal life.*
JOHN 6:47 NIV

A PRAYER

Dear Lord, You have saved me by Your grace. Keep me mindful that Your grace is a gift that I can accept but cannot earn. I praise You, Father, for that priceless gift. Today and every day, let me share the good news of Your grace with my family, with my friends, and with the world. Amen

PART III:

AND WE SHALL ALSO LIVE

"If we have died with Christ, we believe that we shall also live with Him."

ROMANS 6:8 NASB

Christ endured the crown of thorns and the cross at Golgotha so that we might have the gift of eternal life. Now, each of us must claim that gift as our own.

Let us accept the Savior into our hearts. Let us share His good news. Let us obey His commandments. Let us accept His abundance and His peace. Let us pick up our cross and follow Him wherever He may lead. Let us trust Him with our lives, our hearts, and our souls, this day and forever.

8

AND WE SHALL ALSO LIVE

Truly, truly, I say to you, he who hears My word, and believes Him who sent Me, has eternal life, and does not come into judgment, but has passed out of death into life. Truly, truly, I say to you, an hour is coming and now is, when the dead will hear the voice of the Son of God, and those who hear will live.

JOHN 5:24-25 NASB 1995

Outside the city walls of Jerusalem, on a hill called Golgotha, Jesus sacrificed His life on the cross so that we might have life eternal. This gift, freely given from God's only begotten Son, is the priceless possession of everyone who accepts Him as Lord and Savior. Thankfully, grace is not an earthly reward for righteous behavior; it is, instead, a blessed spiritual gift. When we accept Christ into our hearts, we are saved by His grace.

The familiar words from the book of Ephesians make God's promise perfectly clear: "For it is by grace you have been saved, through faith—and this not from yourselves, it is the gift of God—not by works, so that no one can boast" (2:8–9 NIV).

God's grace is the ultimate gift, and we owe to Him the ultimate in thanksgiving. Let us praise the Creator for His priceless gift, and let us share the good news with the world. We return our Father's love by accepting His grace and by sharing His message and His love.

God is waiting patiently for each of us to accept His gift of eternal life. And the next move is ours.

> The crucial question for each of us is this: What do you think of Jesus, and do you yet have a personal acquaintance with Him?
>
> HANNAH WHITALL SMITH

> The seed of God stirred, shoved, and sprouted. The ground trembled, and the rock of the tomb tumbled. And the flower of Easter blossomed.
>
> MAX LUCADO

> Because he lives I can face tomorrow. Because he lives all fear is gone. Because I know he holds the future, and life is worth living, just because he lives.
>
> BILL AND GLORIA GAITHER

Jesus is the personal approach from the unseen God coming so near that he becomes inescapable. You don't have to find him—you just have to consent to be found.

E. Stanly Jones

The secret of the Christian is that he knows the absolute deity of the Lord Jesus Christ.

Oswald Chambers

When we invite Jesus into our lives, we experience life in the fullest, most vital sense.

Catherine Marshall

And because we know Christ is alive, we have hope for the present and hope for life beyond the grave.

Billy Graham

There is so much Heaven around us now if we have eyes for it, because eternity starts when we give ourselves to God.

Gloria Gaither

Easter comes each year to remind us of a truth that is eternal and universal. The empty tomb of Easter morning says to you and me, "Of course you'll encounter trouble. But behold a God of power who can take any evil and turn it into a door of hope."

CATHERINE MARSHALL

Ultimately, our relationship with Christ is
the one thing we cannot do without.
BETH MOORE

Jesus gives us hope because He keeps us company,
has a vision and knows the way we should go.
MAX LUCADO

The earth's troubles fade in the light of heaven's hope.
BILLY GRAHAM

The presence of hope in the invincible
sovereignty of God drives out fear.
JOHN PIPER

Christ is the humility of God embodied in
human nature; the Eternal Love humbling
itself, clothing itself in the garb of meekness
and gentleness, to win and serve and save us.
ANDREW MURRAY

God is and all is well.
JOHN GREENLEAF WHITTIER

For whosoever will save his life shall lose it; but whosoever shall lose his life for my sake and the gospel's, the same shall save it.
MARK 8:35 KJV

But God demonstrates his own love for us in this: While we were still sinners, Christ died for us.
ROMANS 5:8 NIV

A PRAYER

Lord, I am here on this earth for only a brief while. But You have offered me the priceless gift of eternal life through Your Son Jesus. I accept Your gift, Lord, with thanksgiving and praise. And as an expression of my faith in You, let me share the good news of my salvation with those who need Your healing touch. Amen

9

BUILDING UPON THE ROCK

Therefore whosoever heareth these sayings of mine, and doeth them, I will liken him unto a wise man, which built his house upon a rock: and the rain descended, and the floods came, and the winds blew, and beat upon that house; and it fell not: for it was founded upon a rock.

MATTHEW 7:24–25 KJV

God has given us a guidebook for righteous living called the Holy Bible. It contains thorough instructions which, if followed, lead to fulfillment, righteousness, and salvation. But if we choose to ignore God's commandments, the results are as predictable as they are tragic.

A righteous life has many components: faith, honesty, generosity, love, kindness, humility, gratitude, and worship, to name but a few. If we seek to follow the steps of our Savior, Jesus Christ, we must seek to live according to His commandments. In short, we must, to the best of our abilities, live according to the principles contained in God's Holy Word.

> Obedience is the natural outcome of belief.
> C. H. SPURGEON

> Abide in Jesus, the sinless one—which means, give up all of self and its life, and dwell in God's will and rest in His strength. This is what brings the power that does not commit sin.
> ANDREW MURRAY

> A believer comes to Christ; a disciple follows after Him.
> VANCE HAVNER

> If we have the true love of God in our hearts, we will show it in our lives. We will not have to go up and down the earth proclaiming it. We will show it in everything we say or do.
> D. L. MOODY

What is God looking for? He is looking for men
and women whose hearts are completely His.

CHARLES SWINDOLL

We had better quickly discover whether we have
mere religion or a real experience with Jesus,
whether we have outward observance of religious
forms or hearts that beat in tune with God.

JIM CYMBALA

When we are in a situation where Jesus is all we
have, we soon discover he is all we really need.

GIGI GRAHAM TCHIVIDJIAN

Faith expects from God what is beyond all expectation.

ANDREW MURRAY

The Christian life boils down to a battle
of wills: Christ's versus our own.

CHARLES SWINDOLL

Christians see sin for what it is: willful rebellion against the rulership of God in their lives. And in turning from their sin, they have embraced God's only means of dealing with sin: Jesus.

KAY ARTHUR

The Christian life is not a playground; it is a battleground.

WARREN WIERSBE

Keep your face upturned to Christ as the flowers do to the sun. Look, and your soul shall live and grow.

HANNAH WHITALL SMITH

Major on Jesus Christ. Make Him the preeminent One in your life. You have all things *in* Him, *with* Him, and *through* Him—and nothing is greater than that.

WARREN WIERSBE

To be prepared to die is to be prepared
to live; to be ready for eternity is, in the
best sense, to be ready for today.

C. H. SPURGEON

God loves us the way we are, but He loves
us too much to leave us that way.

LEIGHTON FORD

Christ's work of making new men is not mere
improvement, but transformation.

C. S. LEWIS

Grow, dear friends, but grow, I beseech you, in
God's way, which is the only true way.

HANNAH WHITALL SMITH

We can prove our faith by our commitment to it and in no other way. Any belief that does not command the one who holds it is not a real belief—it is only a pseudo-belief.

A. W. TOZER

Where there are no good works, there is no faith. If works and love do not blossom forth, it is not genuine faith, the Gospel has not yet gained a foothold, and Christ is not yet rightly known.

MARTIN LUTHER

It is faith that saves us, not works, but the faith that saves us always produces works.

C. H. SPURGEON

We are saved by faith alone, but faith is never alone.

JOHN CALVIN

Has he taken over your heart? Perhaps he
resides there, but does he preside there?

VANCE HAVNER

Be assured, if you walk with Him and look to Him,
and expect help from Him, He will never fail you.

GEORGE MUELLER

Choose Jesus Christ! Deny yourself, take up the Cross,
and follow Him, for the world must be shown. The world
must see, in us, a discernible, visible, startling difference.

ELISABETH ELLIOT

The heaviest end of the cross lies ever on His shoulders.
If He bids us carry a burden, He carries it also.

C. H. SPURGEON

*And hereby we do know that we know
him, if we keep his commandments.*
1 John 2:3 KJV

Even so faith, if it has no works, it is dead.
James 2:17 NASB 1995

Therefore, since we have this ministry because we were shown mercy, we do not give up. Instead, we have renounced shameful secret things, not walking in deceit or distorting God's message, but commending ourselves to every person's conscience in God's sight by an open display of the truth.
2 Corinthians 4:1-2 HCSB

A PRAYER

Dear Lord, direct my path far from the temptations and distractions of the world. Make me a worthy example to my family and friends. And let my kind words and my good deeds serve as a testimony to the changes You have made in my life. Let me praise You, Father, by following in the footsteps of Your Son, and let others see Him through me. Amen

10

THE ABUNDANT LIFE

*I have come that they may have life, and
that they may have it more abundantly.*

John 10:10 NKJV

God's Word promises that His abundance is available to each of us. He offers His blessings, but He doesn't force them upon us. To receive them, we must trust His promises and we must follow, as closely as we can, in the footsteps of His Son. But the world tempts us to do otherwise.

The world tempts us to descend into fits of pessimism and doubt. And the world bombards us with a never ending assortment of time-squandering distractions and wallet-draining temptations.

Everywhere you turn, someone or something is vying for your attention, trying to convince you that peace and happiness are commodities that can be purchased for the right price. But buyer beware. Genuine peace and spiritual abundance are not for sale at any price. In truth, real abundance is never obtained through power, through prestige, or through worldly possessions. Genuine abundance results from your relationship with God and His only begotten Son. No exceptions.

Do you sincerely seek the abundant life that Jesus promises in John 10:10? Then turn your life and your heart over to Him. When you do, you'll receive the love, the peace, and the abundance that that can come only from the touch of the Master's hand.

> God is the giver, and we are the receivers. And His richest gifts are bestowed not upon those who do the greatest things, but upon those who accept His abundance and His grace.
>
> HANNAH WHITALL SMITH

> God loves you and wants you to experience peace and life—abundant and eternal.
>
> BILLY GRAHAM

> We honor God by asking for great things when they are a part of His promise. We dishonor Him and cheat ourselves when we ask for molehills where He has promised mountains.
>
> VANCE HAVNER

Knowing that your future is absolutely assured
can free you to live abundantly today.

SARAH YOUNG

Jesus wants Life for us; Life with a capital L.

JOHN ELDREDGE

Joy is the direct result of having God's perspective on
our daily lives and the effect of loving our Lord enough
to obey His commands and trust His promises.

BILL BRIGHT

Joy is the settled assurance that God is in control of
all the details of my life, the quiet confidence that
ultimately everything is going to be all right, and
the determined choice to praise God in all things.

KAY WARREN

Joy is the serious business of heaven.

C. S. LEWIS

And God is able to make all grace abound to you, so that always having all sufficiency in everything, you may have an abundance for every good deed.
2 CORINTHIANS 9:8 NASB

My cup runs over. Surely goodness and mercy shall follow me all the days of my life; and I will dwell in the house of the LORD forever.
PSALM 23:5–6 NKJV

May Yahweh bless you and protect you; may Yahweh make His face shine on you and be gracious to you.
NUMBERS 6:24–25 HCSB

A PRAYER

Dear Lord, the peace that the world offers is fleeting, but You offer a peace that is perfect and eternal. I am grateful for the abundant life that is mine through Your Son. Grant me the wisdom to claim His blessings. And lead me on Your path, Father, now and forever. Amen

11

ULTIMATE PEACE

The peace of God, which surpasses all understanding, will guard your hearts and minds through Christ Jesus.

Philippians 4:7 NKJV

Peace. It's such a beautiful word. It conveys images of serenity, contentment, and freedom from the trials and tribulations of everyday existence. Peace means freedom from conflict, freedom from inner turmoil, and freedom from worry. The world promises its own brand of peace, a peace that is for sale to the highest bidders. But contrary to the implied claims of modern media, real peace —genuine peace that lasts—isn't for sale. At any price.

Have you discovered the genuine peace that can be yours through Christ? Or are you still scurrying after the illusion of peace that the world promises but cannot deliver? If you've turned things over to Jesus, you'll be blessed now and forever. But if you're still struggling with distractions and distortions that interfere with your ability to follow ever more closely in Christ's footsteps, perhaps this the day to claim—or reclaim—the peace that is rightfully yours: His peace.

Let Jesus rule your heart and your thoughts, beginning now. When you do, you'll experience the peace that only He can give.

> Only Christ can meet the deepest needs of our world and our hearts. Christ alone can bring lasting peace.
> BILLY GRAHAM

> In the center of a hurricane there is absolute quiet and peace. There is no safer place than in the center of the will of God.
> CORRIE TEN BOOM

> Deep within the center of the soul is a chamber of peace where God lives and where, if we will enter it and quiet all the other sounds, we can hear His gentle whisper.
> LETTIE COWMAN

> God's power is great enough for our deepest desperation. You can go on. You can pick up the pieces and start anew. You can face your fears. You can find peace in the rubble. There is healing for your soul.
> SUZANNE DALE EZELL

Peace does not mean to be in a place where there is no noise, trouble, or hard work. Peace means to be in the midst of all those things and still be calm in your heart.

CATHERINE MARSHALL

Meditating upon His Word will inevitably bring peace of mind, strength of purpose, and power for living.

BILL BRIGHT

God's peace is like a river, not a pond. In other words, a sense of health and well-being, both of which are expressions of the Hebrew shalom, can permeate our homes even when we're in white-water rapids.

BETH MOORE

Where the soul is full of peace and joy, outward surroundings and circumstances are of comparatively little account.

HANNAH WHITALL SMITH

What peace can they have who are not at peace with God?

MATTHEW HENRY

Jesus did not die on the cross just so we could live comfortable, well-adjusted lives. His purpose is far deeper: He wants to make us like Himself before He takes us to heaven. This is our greatest privilege, our immediate responsibility, and our ultimate destiny.

RICK WARREN

These things I have spoken to you, that in Me you may have peace. In the world you will have tribulation; but be of good cheer, I have overcome the world.
John 16:33 NKJV

Peace I leave with you, My peace I give to you; not as the world gives do I give to you. Let not your heart be troubled, neither let it be afraid.
JOHN 14:27 NKJV

He Himself is our peace.
EPHESIANS 2:14 NASB

But the fruit of the Spirit is love, joy, peace, patience, kindness, goodness, faith, gentleness, self-control. Against such things there is no law.
GALATIANS 5:22–23 HCSB

A PRAYER

Dear Lord, I thank You for the priceless gift of life and for Your infinite love. You give me a sense of peace that the world can never provide. I thank You, Father, for Your love, for Your peace, and for Your Son. Amen

12

SHARING THE GOOD NEWS

Now then we are ambassadors for Christ.

2 CORINTHIANS 5:20 KJV

After His resurrection, Jesus addressed his disciples: *But the eleven disciples proceeded to Galilee, to the mountain which Jesus had designated. When they saw Him, they worshiped Him; but some were doubtful. And Jesus came up and spoke to them, saying, "All authority has been given to Me in heaven and on earth. Go therefore and make disciples of all the nations, baptizing them in the name of the Father and the Son and the Holy Spirit, teaching them to observe all that I commanded you; and lo, I am with you always, even to the end of the age."*

MATTHEW 28:16–20 NASB 1995

Christ's great commission applies to Christians of every generation, including our own. As believers, we are called to share the good n ews of Jesus Christ with our families, with our neighbors, and with the world. Jesus commanded His disciples to become fishers of men. We must do likewise, and we must do so today. Tomorrow may indeed be too late.

> Our commission is quite specific. We are told to be His witness to all nations. For us, as His disciples, to refuse any part of this commission frustrates the love of Jesus Christ, the Son of God.
> CATHERINE MARSHALL

> I look upon all the world as my parish.
> JOHN WESLEY

> Jesus made Himself known to His own, and if others are to hear about Him today, you and I must tell them.
> VANCE HAVNER

> God is not saving the world; it is done. Our business is to get men and women to realize it.
> OSWALD CHAMBERS

Go. This is the command of our Lord. Where? To the world, for it is the world that is on God's heart. Out there are multitudes for whom Christ died. And the minute you and I receive the light of the gospel, we, at that moment, become responsible for spreading that light to those who are still in darkness. Granted, we cannot all go physically, but we can go on our knees.

KAY ARTHUR

Apostles are made from common men.

LETTIE COWMAN

Christ is our temple, in whom by faith all believers meet.

MATTHEW HENRY

You can go to the mission field in person, by prayer, by provision, or by proxy. But remember, there is a mission field across the street as well as across the sea.

VANCE HAVNER

Christ is with us . . . and the warmth is contagious.

JONI EARECKSON TADA

His voice leads us not into timid
discipleship but into bold witness.

CHARLES STANLEY

If we understand what lies ahead for those
who do not know Christ, there will be a
sense of urgency in our witness.

DAVID JEREMIAH

God had only one Son, and He was a missionary.

DAVID LIVINGSTONE

When your heart is ablaze with the love of God,
then you love other people—especially the
sinners—so much that you dare to tell them
about Jesus with no apologies and no fear.

CATHERINE MARSHALL

Shout the shout of faith. Nothing can withstand the
triumphant faith that links itself to omnipotence. For
"this is the victory that overcometh the world." The
secret of all successful living lies in this shout of faith.

HANNAH WHITALL SMITH

Do not go to an Easter service to hear the best news in the world without bringing someone with you who needs to hear it for the first time.

RICK WARREN

You are the light of the world. A city set on a hill cannot be hidden; nor does anyone light a lamp and put it under a basket, but on the lampstand, and it gives light to all who are in the house. Let your light shine before men in such a way that they may see your good works, and glorify your Father who is in heaven.

MATTHEW 5:14–16 NASB 1995

You are a chosen people. You are royal priests, a holy nation, God's very own possession. As a result, you can show others the goodness of God, for he called you out of the darkness into his wonderful light.

1 PETER 2:9 NLT

I will also make You a light of the nations so that My salvation may reach to the end of the earth.

ISAIAH 49:6 NASB

A PRAYER

Heavenly Father, every man and woman, every boy and girl is Your child. You desire that all Your children know Jesus as their Lord and Savior. Father, let me be part of Your Great Commission. Let me give, let me pray, and let me go out into this world so that I might be a fisher of men *for You*. Amen

13

A TIME FOR CELEBRATION

The stone the builders rejected has become the cornerstone. the LORD has done this, and it is marvelous in our eyes. The LORD has done it this very day; let us rejoice today and be glad.

PSALM 118:22–24 NIV

The 118th Psalm reminds us that today, like every other day, is a cause for celebration. God gives us this day; He fills it to the brim with possibilities, and He challenges us to use it for His purposes. The day is presented to us fresh and clean at midnight, free of charge, but we must beware: today is a nonrenewable resource—once it's gone, it's gone forever. Our responsibility, of course, is to use this day in the service of God's will and according to His commandments.

Today, as you consider the meaning of the cross and the implications of the empty tomb, give thanks for Christ *and* for the priceless gift of eternal life. Give the Father the glory, the praise, and the thanksgiving that He deserves. And search for the hidden possibilities that God has placed along your path. This day is a priceless gift from your heavenly Father. Use it joyfully and encourage others to do likewise. After all, this is the day the Lord has made.

> God is the giver, and we are the receivers. And His richest gifts are bestowed not upon those who do the greatest things, but upon those who accept His abundance and His grace.
> HANNAH WHITALL SMITH

> We may often forget to meditate on the perfection of our Lord, but He never ceases to remember us.
> C. H. SPURGEON

> There is not one blade of grass, there is no color in this world that is not intended to make us rejoice.
> JOHN CALVIN

> How changed our lives would be if we could only fly through the days on wings of surrender and trust!
> HANNAH WHITALL SMITH

The Lord is glad to open the gate to every knocking soul.
It opens very freely; its hinges are not rusted; no bolts
secure it. Have faith and enter at this moment through
holy courage. If you knock with a heavy heart, you
shall yet sing with joy of spirit. Never be discouraged!

C. H. SPURGEON

Our hope in Christ for the future is
the mainstream of our joy.

C. H. SPURGEON

Those who are God's without reserve
are, in every sense, content.

HANNAH WHITALL SMITH

Have your heart right with Christ, and he will visit you
often, and so turn weekdays into Sundays, meals into
sacraments, homes into temples, and earth into heaven.

C. H. SPURGEON

*Rejoice in the Lord always.
I will say it again: Rejoice!*
Philippians 4:4 HCSB

Rejoice evermore. Pray without ceasing. In every thing give thanks: for this is the will of God in Christ Jesus concerning you.
1 Thessalonians 5:16–18 KJV

So now we can rejoice in our wonderful new relationship with God because our Lord Jesus Christ has made us friends of God.
Romans 5:11 NLT

A PRAYER

Dear Lord, You have given me so many reasons to celebrate. Today, let me choose an attitude of cheerfulness. Let me be a joyful Christian, Father, quick to laugh and slow to anger. And let me share Your goodness with my family, my friends, and my neighbors, this day and every day. Amen

14

A TIME FOR PRAISE

The LORD is my strength and my defense; he has become my salvation. He is my God, and I will praise him.

EXODUS 15:2 NIV

As we consider Christ's sacrifice on the cross and His resurrection, we are humbled by His love. And because we owe Christ so much, we must praise Him with our prayers, with our words, and with our deeds.

Lettie Cowman, the author of the classic devotional text *Streams in the Desert*, wrote, "Two wings are necessary to lift our souls toward God: prayer and praise. Prayer asks. Praise accepts the answer."

Today, carve out a few moments to count your blessings *and* celebrate them. And every time you notice a gift from the Giver of all things good, praise Him. His works are marvelous, His gifts are beyond understanding, and His love endures forever.

The time for universal praise is sure to come
some day. Let us begin to do our part now.
HANNAH WHITALL SMITH

Preoccupy my thoughts with your praise beginning today.
JONI EARECKSON TADA

It is only with gratitude that life becomes rich.
DIETRICH BONHOEFFER

No part of our prayers creates a greater feeling of
joy than when we praise God for who He is. He is our
Master Creator, our Father, our source of all love.
SHIRLEY DOBSON

When there is peace in the heart,
there will be praise on the lips.
WARREN WIERSBE

It's our privilege to not only raise our hands in
worship but also to combine the visible with
the invisible in a rising stream of praise and
adoration sent directly to our Father.

SHIRLEY DOBSON

Praise and thank God for who He is and
for what He has done for you.

BILLY GRAHAM

This is my story, this is my song,
praising my Savior, all the day long.

FANNY CROSBY

Inside the human heart is an undeniable,
spiritual instinct to commune with its Creator.

JIM CYMBALA

Spiritual worship is focusing all we are on all He is.
BETH MOORE

Thanksgiving or complaining—these words express two contrastive attitudes of the souls of God's children in regard to His dealings with them. The soul that gives thanks can find comfort in everything; the soul that complains can find comfort in nothing.
HANNAH WHITALL SMITH

My soul, hearken to the voice of your God. He is always ready to speak with you when you are prepared to hear. If there is any slowness to commune, it is not on His part but altogether on your own. He stands at the door and knocks, and if His people will only open, He rejoices to enter.
C. H. SPURGEON

Though we cannot by our prayers give God any information, yet we must by our prayers give him honor.
MATTHEW HENRY

God meant for life to be filled with joy and purpose.
He invites us to take our journey with Him.

BILLY GRAHAM

Christianity, in its purest form, is nothing
more than seeing Jesus. Christian service, in
its purest form, is nothing more than imitating
him who we see. To see his Majesty and to
imitate him: that is the sum of Christianity.

MAX LUCADO

Faith is not merely you holding on to
God—it is God holding on to you.

E. STANLEY JONES

The last and greatest lesson that the soul has to learn
is the fact that God, and God alone, is enough for
all its needs. This is the lesson that all His dealings
with us are meant to teach; and this is the crowning
discovery of our whole Christian life. God is enough!

HANNAH WHITALL SMITH

*God lifted him high and honored him far
beyond anyone or anything, ever, so that all
created beings in heaven and on earth—even
those long ago dead and buried—will bow
in worship before this Jesus Christ, and call
out in praise that he is the Master of all, to
the glorious honor of God the Father.*

PHILIPPIANS 2:9–11 MSG

*But now in Christ Jesus you who formerly
were far off have been brought near by the
blood of Christ. For He Himself is our peace.*

EPHESIANS 2:13–14 NASB 1995

Be still, and know that I am God.

PSALM 46:10 KJV

*I can do all things through Christ
which strengtheneth me.*

PHILIPPIANS 4:13 KJV

*A time is coming and has now come
when the true worshipers will worship
the Father in the Spirit and in truth, for
they are the kind of worshipers the Father
seeks. God is spirit, and his worshipers
must worship in the Spirit and in truth.*
John 4:23-24 NIV

*Finally, brethren, whatever is true, whatever
is honorable, whatever is right, whatever is
pure, whatever is lovely, whatever is of good
repute, if there is any excellence and if anything worthy of praise, dwell on these things.*
Philippians 4:8 NASB 1995

*For God so loved the world, that he gave his
only begotten Son, that whosoever believeth in
him should not perish, but have everlasting life.*
John 3:16 KJV

A PRAYER

Heavenly Father, Your gifts are greater than I can imagine, and Your love for me is greater than I can fathom. May I live each day with thanksgiving in my heart and praise on my lips. Thank You for the gift of Your Son and for the promise of eternal life. Let me share the joyous news of Jesus Christ with a world that needs His healing touch this day and every day. Amen

HE IS RISEN!